My Little Book of

Burrowing Owls

By Hope Irvin Marston

Illustrated by Maria Magdalena Brown

NORTHWORD

NorthWord Press, Inc.
Minocqua, Wisconsin

One spring evening, two burrowing owls skimmed over the grasslands. Down they dropped to an empty prairie dog burrow.

They crept inside
and looked around their old nest.
Another animal had lived in it
over the winter, and it was a mess.

The owls would clean it up.

The busy little birds pecked at the walls with their beaks.

SWISH! SWISH!

The male bird kicked the dirt backward toward the burrow opening. Out flew little puffs of dirt.

When the owl stopped to rest,
his mate finished the cleaning.

That night, the owls stood on the mound outside the burrow. They bent their gangly legs and bowed to each other.

"Cu-coo. Cu-coo," sang the male.

The owls snuggled throughout the night.
Sometimes they rubbed each other's bills.
And they preened each other's feathers.
When the male saw a field mouse in the grass,
he brought it to his mate for a midnight snack.

The next day the owls lined their nest with feathers
and dead grass. And with dried cow manure.

They left some manure outside the burrow.
The smell would help keep hungry badgers
or snakes away from their babies.

During the next two weeks the female laid seven eggs.
She turned the eggs often to keep them warm beneath her.
Twice a day she hopped up to the entrance for food.

"Rasssp! Rasssp!" She called to her mate.

He flew to her with insects. Or birds. Or mice.

The first egg
hatched on the
twenty-eighth day.

Day after day
another little owlet
no bigger than your
thumb pipped
its shell.

Each of the seven
helpless new
owlets opened its
eyes when
it was five
days old.

When the owlets were about two weeks old, they hobbled out of the crowded burrow. They huddled in the bright sunlight near the entrance.

"Kook-COO!"

"Kook-COO!"

They called, like tiny roosters trying to crow.

They wanted to be fed.

Down swooped their father
with a small garter snake. The owlets
rushed at him on their spindly legs.

They grabbed the snake from his beak and gobbled it up.

The parents worked hard finding food
for the hungry little chicks.

When they were three
weeks old, the owlets could run.

And hop.

And preen.

And flap their wings.

It was time to learn to hunt
for their own food.

Their father taught them
to catch grasshoppers and other bugs.

One morning the owlets
sat in the sun near the burrow.
Suddenly, the mother owl
began to bob her body.
She swiveled her head.

"Tweee-chikit-
chikit-
chikit- chik!"
she warned.

A fox
was creeping,
closer and closer.

"Eep! Eep! Eep!"
cried the owlets as they hurried
into the burrow. Their mother
rushed in right behind them.

As the fox came toward the burrow,
it heard,

"HisssZZZZ! HisssZZZZZZZ! HISSSZZZZZ!"

It sounded like a rattlesnake. The fox turned and ran back across the prairie. The little owls had scared the fox away. It didn't know frightened burrowing owls hissed like rattlesnakes.

When it was safe, the owlets came out of the burrow.

They s-t-r-e-t-c-h-e-d themselves.
They chased beetles and bugs and crickets.
They flapped their wings.
They made funny little leaps into the air,
but they couldn't fly yet.

The owls did learn to fly by the time they were six
weeks old. Still, they stayed near the burrow.
They perched on fence posts
to watch for prey on the ground.

They flew over the grass in search
of grasshoppers. Or locusts. Or dragonflies.
When they found some,
they grabbed them with their talons.

The parent owls sat on the ground
and fluffed their feathers. They pushed
their faces into the loose soil
and swiveled their heads,
scattering the dirt.

By bathing in the dust, they got rid of loose feathers. And fleas. And mites. Soon the seven owlets were dust bathing too.

As the owlets grew, their nest became too crowded. One by one they moved into empty burrows of their own nearby.

One fall morning, frost covered the ground.
A cold wind blew.

The owls had trouble finding food.
It was time to leave the northern prairie.
Now they must fly south to warm weather. And lizards. And bugs.
In the spring they would return to raise families of their own.

DEDICATION
For Arthur

Special Thanks to Denver W. Holt and Kila Jarvis
of the Owl Research Institute, Inc., Missoula, Montana.

© Hope Irvin Marston, 1996
Illustrations © Maria Magdalena Brown, 1996

NORTHWORD PRESS, INC.
P.O. Box 1360
Minocqua, WI 54548

Designed by Amy J. Monday

Library of Congress Cataloging-in-Publication Data

Marston, Hope Irvin.
        My little book of burrowing owls / by Hope Irvin Marston;
illustrations by Maria Magdalena Brown.
        p.   cm.
        Summary: Explains how burrowing owls raise their young.
        ISBN 1-55971-547-2 (sc)
   1. Burrowing owl—Juvenile literature.   2. Burrowing owl—Infancy—Juvenile literature.
   [1. Burrowing owl.   2. Owls.]   I. Brown, Maria Magdelena, ill. II. Title.
    QL696.S83M324 1996
     598.9'7--dc20   95-36480

Printed in Malaysia